She's not the boss of me.....

Of course she is who am I kidding?

H.S. *Smiles*

Foreword

H.S. Smiles' latest poetry collection is equal parts raw grit and lust, versus a sizzling pan fire helping of pure romantic passion. The woman of which he speaks to and speaks of in all his works has been built up and placed on a pedestal, like she's the ideal relationship entity that the author wishes for in his mind. She may not be the boss of him and he not the boss of her, but she also is the boss of him in a way that she grounds him and makes him swim around in a lake filled with swans that's surrounded by heart shaped tree hedges along the perimeter. There's a pure sense of bubbly romantic bliss to be found in these poems, even the ones that ride way off the wild rails and straight into the bedroom. Solo's works have evolved since his original publications and he becomes more compassionate and starry-eyed with each passing micro poem. There's a little bit of something for every poetry aficionado found within these pages and by the time the back cover closes, you'll have a satisfied grin on your face that says *if this couple wasn't made for their own unfurling ages, then I'm sure they'd be much better off alone.* Ross had Rachel, Monica had Chandler, but these two characters share a blossomed complexity that makes sense both entirely to themselves and to any curious readers.

Eric Keegan author of
"A Declaration of our Rippling Days"
Instagram: @blankpagesofmine

Contents

She's Poetry...

She's not the boss of me.
Who am I kidding....?

Of course she is
when she wants to be.

She had a gift.

A certain talent
a beautiful mind

and quite the
spectacular ass!!

*Let's make love
at the end of
the rainbow.
As you princess
are my little
pot of gold!*

*She's as fierce
and feisty
as she is caring
and empathetic.*

*We came to dance
and cause nothing
but such absolutely
wonderful trouble.*

*She asked him
what he'd wished for.
Closing his eyes whilst
kissing her deeply,
he whispered....
"I'd wish for you"*

When she's always
on your mind
those 2am thoughts
will always be
welcome at 2pm.

*Sure she's beautiful
when she's mad
but I think she's
gorgeous in all
her moods, so
much so I can't
take my eyes off
her anyway.*

*I love the moments
where there is nothing
but mischief deep
within her eyes,
and nothing but charm
in that sweet yet not so
innocent smile.*

And like a perfect storm
she came into my life
turned it on its head
and stayed.
And I couldn't be
more grateful.

I love the way she thinks
as much as I love the way
she flicks her hair and shakes
her ass like she's won.
Even more so when I know
she knows she is wrong.

I fell for the girl
with wonder
in her eyes, and
that pretty cute
yet inquisitive mind.

*I swear that her
empathetic heart
will save the world.
I mean......
how could it not?!?*

She held my heart
carefully, plucking
and strumming at
the strings ensuring
that it sang just for her.

*Every day my
heart whispers
"Fuck, there she is"
is always a great day.*

*She's not high maintenance
she just knows her worth
and true value so she has
lost the ability to settle
for anything less.*

She could turn
a phrase as
quickly as she
could turn a page,
and that's why I
fell in love with a writer.

*She's always there
at the back of my mind
reminding me of who
I'm doing it for
from time to time.*

*Her weird
matches mine.*

*God help the
rest of ya.*

She was a natural,
empathetic and
charismatic, quite
a sight to behold.

She was an angel in blue
jeans and converse,
a sultry temptress with
an appetite for pleasure
whether it was yours or hers.

She was the kinda girl
who deserved the world
and yes I was going
to give it to her.

She was enchanting
enticing and alluring.
She was a temptress
dressed to impress
wearing nothing
but her heart on
her sleeve, and that
delicious and
decadent smile.

*She wears white
as if it's the only
light the world
could ever need.*

*There's this girl
and she has the
ability to turn
the hard and
the smart into
melty ass goofballs.*

*She's glamorous
and fabulous
and that's before
she applies her
war paint.*

*She's not meant
to be tamed or caged.*

*She needs not your
permission to do
her thing.*

So ride or die fucker.

Ride with her wild or die.

Close your eyes
take a deep breath
and realise that she
is indeed a hurricane
wrapped in a little
black dress and her
tone will always sound
sultry even when her
words are scathing
as they leave her
alluring lips

*Oh you could tell
that girl was trouble
from the way she
carried herself
right to that melty
making giggle.*

She could be sat with
her hair up
no makeup
and wearing
nothing but
my hoody,
and I'd still
think she is the
most ravishing
girl in the world.

If those alluring eyes
and wonderful smile
don't hook you in
that magnificent
mind of hers
truly will.

So yeah,
last night
I went to this
girls yard
and all I got
was a lousy
milkshake.

*You've got to
keep your eyes
on that one.
She's as cute
as she is fierce
and has no qualms
with saying
thank you in
quite a naughty way.*

*Sure she can be
stubborn
yes she's pretty
fucking feral,
but to me she's
irresistible and
absolutely irreplaceable.*

*If she wants to
help the Empire
to destroy
 a rebel base!*

Guess what

*we're going to
kill some rebels.*

*I found out she
had a dark side
and I couldn't help
but want to be
her apprentice.*

*At 3am every
single heartbeat
sounds like it's
whispering her name.*

Walk with me in
the storm and along
the shore darling.
We'll skip stones
into the ocean and
cause such a gentle
tidal wave.

*She isn't chaos incarnate
she just doesn't tolerate
any fucking bullshit.*

Tell me darling.
Oh tell me what
it will take for
you to realise it's
not a mistake
to believe in yourself.

*She looks like a goddess
whilst wearing my
flannel shirts.*

*Yet I look like some
hipster fucking
lumberjack
when I wear them.*

She's beautiful in
black and ravishing
in red and that soul
of hers is so damn
alluring when it's
laid bare for all to see.

I fell for the girl
with a warrior soul
a badass heart
and the morals of
an alley cat.

When I'm in her arms
and lost in her eyes
I can't help but feel
like I'm floating on
a breeze and I never
want to come down.

There's this girl
and the only
tolerance she
has for pricks
are the ones that
comes from a
tattoo gun.

*She would turn heads
melt hearts and take
your breath away.*

All before breakfast!

*I wasn't convinced
that angels could
walk among us
until I met her!*

*SHE WOULD DO
AS SHE IS TOLD....*

*BUT SHE HAS A
BRAIN AND A
BACKBONE*

SO......

FUCK YOU!

She has a country girl smile,
a punk rock attitude,
and those hips, well they could
be best described as good
old fashioned rock n roll.

*She knew what it
was like to be hated
yet had the strength
to show the world
how big her heart
had grown, and how
far it had come.*

Gazing into her
beautiful hazel eyes
I watched as her
cheeks redden.
Yearning to hold them
in my hands,
cupping gently as our
lips met softly.

Lost in the moment...

Catching her breath in mine
a second lasts a minute
turning into a lifetime
our hearts beat together
as she becomes mine
and I become hers.

*Her flaws may
seem like a
curse to her
but trust me
when I say
she's a blessing
to me in
every way.*

She has the
wildest thoughts
wild and messy hair
and the widest smile
I have ever seen.

*In a world
misunderstood
and filled with chaos.*

*She came to be
the only thing to
make perfect sense.*

*If you say she's
a girl you would
die for....
your Google search
should match that energy.*

*Personally
I search for shit
so she doesn't
have to.*

*I fell for
the girl with
the wind in
her hair and
sand in her toes.
I fell for
the girl with a
rebellious soul
and a reckless heart
so much so that
I fell for her whole.*

I found parts of her
in every song I
listened to, caught
in the grooves of
my heart.
Her slender fingers
pluck tenderly
at my heart strings
allowing us both to
sing loudly of our
adoration for each other.

I found her where
the wild roses grow
reading
relaxing
baring her naked
soul to a world
not quite ready
for such a
delicious vision.

*She's the type
to bring a knife
to a gun fight
and be the only
one left to
walk out alive.*

*From the moment
we met I knew
you were the girl
my mother warned
me about and
my father would
absolutely adore.*

*She's the muse
that poets would
write about
as soon as she
allows them
to leave the bedroom*

*And just like that
she NAMA'd the
fuck out of that STE.*

She's as feisty
as she is cute
and I'm not sure
if I should find
that to be annoying
or should I be
falling head first
in love.

*She had a
heart of GOLD
a SILVER tongue
and a shiny
PLATINUM soul.*

*She was double
the trouble
yet triple the fun.*

We talk of soul mates
like they only belong
to this lifetime.
But what if they span
multiple lifetimes?
And we actually
made love beneath
the Eiffel Tower
in 1865?

*She was born
to raise hell
and by fuck
did she raise
that particular bar.*

She was chaos
wrapped in
raven hair
red lips and
pale skin.
I couldn't help
but gaze deeply
into her hazel eyes
and feel my chaos
grow within.

All is fair
in love and war
but that ass
gives her
one hell of
an advantage.

She may have
a stamp but
she's not a tramp
nope, that girl
is classy as fuck.

*She didn't think
she could change
the world but
little did she know
that she had a hand
in changing mine.*

She was as rare
as a rose found
growing in concrete
and twice as beautiful

*It's on the days
where she finds
it hard to love
herself where
I step up and
love her twice
as hard.*

Yesss queen....
Stretch marks are sexy
you're exactly like
a tiger that's earned
those stunning and
pretty alluring stripes.

*She's the girl who
says she'll be good
when she meets
your family*

*but she already
knows that she's
not going to be.*

*Her soul unravelled as
her hair was wrapped
around his fingers,
feeling vulnerable
yet taken care of.
She had once known
darkness intimately
and he knew this.
With that knowledge
he would never take
her for granted.
However he would
love her deeply and
show her exactly what
had been missing all along.*

She is the
epitome of
perfection!
Flaws and all

*She's as chaotic
as she's cute
a complex
contradiction
wrapped in
what I only
could describe as
my dream girl.*

*She was a
tidal wave
when all
you wanted
was a dip
in the ocean.*

She lived for the storm as she knew that the chaos it brings would soothe her savage soul.

*Not only would
she wash that
man right out
of her hair,
she would bleach
it, colour it, and
treat herself to
one of those
sexpot not
giving a fuck
kinda hair cuts.*

*If I were to make
a list of Top 5
smiles....*

*Hers would be
the only one on it.*

Sure she's beautiful
when the vibes
are good.

But man...

you should see her
when the vibes
are GREAT

When she has the
weight of the world
upon her shoulders
I offer and give her
mine as I could never
let her carry such
a burden alone.

*There may be a
sweet innocence
hiding behind
those enticing eyes
but that heart
my friends
is nothing but wid.*

She said
"LET THERE BE LIGHT"
and believe it or not
my darkness fucked off

*She was such
a pretty little
rule breaker
with a beauty
I had only read
about in those
stories my
father would
read to me
as a child.*

*There is so much beauty
in this world....
A glorious sunrise
a butterfly's wings
the shimmer of a
lake under the moon
every single tattoo
that I have ever seen
and
HER!!*

*Her name may
have stayed the same
but that timid
little girl she
used to be
sure has changed.*

There's a plethora
of scars on that
gentle heart of hers
yet she still finds
the strength to
be as loving and
as caring as much
as she can.

*I found a subtle
beauty in the way
she would fix herself
like the badass
she is every day.*

They speak of love
like it doesn't exist.
But I've seen it
and I've screamed
her name!!!

*Where some may
just be a footnote
she's the type
of girl that will
be responsible
for you writing
the entire book.*

*She didn't believe
in aliens or unicorns
until she met the one
that proved that
love had existed
all along.*

She may throw
a fuck tonne of shade
but she also has
a shit load of love to give.

A HEART LIKE HERS
BELONGS IN
THE LOUVRE
SO BE CAREFUL
WHEN YOU
HANDLE IT.

Fuck.
She's so sexy
when she is
comfortable
enough to be
vulnerable.

The eyes are a
window to the soul
yet when I gaze
warmly into hers
all I can feel
is at home.

Tell me darling...
Tell me what songs you play
that remind you of me?
Tell me what books do you like
to read to relax
at the end of the day?
Tell me what dreams that you
have that I could help make
come true...
Oh darling why don't
you pour yourself a drink
and tell me everything.
What do you say

She is poetry!
She is poetry!
She is poetry!
She is...
Yup, you've guessed it
she is poetry!

She's Passion...

*Why settle for
the mundane
sweetheart?
You deserve
a magical romance
and some pretty
intense orgasms.*

*She said she would
rip out my throat
and eat me alive*

*I said "Oh darling,
don't you dare threaten
me with a good time."*

She had me
wrapped around
her little finger
as her hair was
wrapped in my fist.

There's so much
I could say about
her smart ass ways
and that smart mouth
of hers, but they say
so much about her
already.

*She sure is beautiful
when she's being bratty.*

*Once upon a time
there was this girl
that decided she
didn't give a fuck
about what other
people thought of her,
and that she obviously
didn't need saving,
thus she would live
happily ever after.*

Her eyes alluring
that smile captivating
her mind fascinating
that subtle seduction
sweet and intoxicating.

*Just because she has
your neck in her teeth
it doesn't mean she
likes you.*

*She could just be hungry
and tired of your shit.*

*She had me where
she wanted as her
face was buried in
my chest, my hand
lost in her raven mane,
and her fingers gently
caressing and teasing
my neck.*

*Bite me anywhere
you please princess.
I'm pretty sure that
if you do I'll quite
like being on my knees.*

Her voice may sound fierce
but when she looks at me
with those big beautiful eyes
I know she wants me to take
her gently whilst seducing her
heart, soul, and mind.

*Her cherry lips
aren't trouble.
But that tongue most
definitely is.*

*Her soul has
seen some shit.
Yet she still smiles.*

Yup.

She's dangerous

I wear her mark
like it's the only
thing that matters
right here deep down
within my hopeful
and romantic heart.

*There's this girl
who can make
me melt just as
much as she
makes me hard.*

Sure she's beautiful
in leather and denim.

But have you seen
her in a corset
and fishnets.......

FUCK ME!

*She was born
and raised as a
sultry contradiction*

*with her approachable
eyes and one helluva
fuck you in her smile.*

She loved autumn
so much that
when the leaves fell
so did her panties.

*She may have
a voice so pure,
but I can't help
wondering what
it would sound like
when she succumbs
to thoughts impure.*

*Given half the chance
she'll leave you
shivering quivering
and spell bound.
Enchanted.
Intoxicated.
Addicted and
Yearning for one
more kiss.*

A night with her
would end with
bloody lips
bruised hips
teeth marks
scratch marks
and a trashed
hotel room whilst
leaving you spent
and craving to do
it over and over again.

The big bad wolf
wouldn't stand a
chance when she
was in that kind
of mood....

You could blow
down her door
but by fuck would
she blow your mind
as you blow your load.

*I could say her
eyes were innocent
but I'd be lying
as it's her mind
that wakes up the
gentle beast in me.*

*I could try and
tame and restrain
her, but when she's
in that mood it's
better to lie back
and enjoy how wild
she can feverishly be.*

*I took a dip
within her
oceans and
might have
left as a
quivering puddle.*

Go get em kitten.
The world is your
playground and
my heart is your
ball of string.

*A spanking is
only used as
a punishment
for when she's
been a bad girl.*

*But truth be told
it is often used as
her reward.*

*She's as reserved
as she is raunchy*

*and you've just
got to respect that!*

Make her laugh
vigorously
and her heart
cum ferociously.

*She whispered
goodnight to
the moon*

*and in the
next breath
devoured me whole.*

*There may be
panic in the streets
but with a girl like her
there's a chaotic calm
to be found inside her
petals and underneath
her silk sheets*

*A lioness is meant
to hunt and protect
her young*

*so why the fuck would
you want to domesticate her?*

*I can't help but
love the look of
her glistening skin
after a night of
romance laughter
and what some would
consider sin.*

Awwwwwwww

*Look at her being
all the shy and shit.*

*With that coy smile
and twinkle in her eye*

*I know that she'll
be having her way
with me later.*

There's this girl
and yup....
she tastes just as
good as she looks.

*She may find herself
on the naughty list
but she doesn't care
as she always gets
her own way
anyway*

*She may like it rough
but she melts just as
much to a gentle yet
firm touch.*

She's the girl
with the ability
to make me forget
my name whilst
I fill the room
with the sound of hers.

*There's just something
about the way she
scratches the shit
out of me that I
kinda like.*

She had a lust
for the finer things
in life but absolutely
loved it when they would
do that pleasure filled
sinful thing she liked.

*Oh what a beautiful mess
she would be
in leather and lace and
wrapped around me.*

*I'm a sucker for
her lip stain on
my lips and collar.*

*I yearn for nights filled
with spontaneous and
unexpected kisses whilst
she's wrapped in my arms.
Lying by the fire acting
like her protector and lover.*

*I long for nights filled
with comfortable silence
communicating through subtle
licks nibbles and winks.*

*I ache for those times our heart
beats as one intimate and
electric whilst quivering
at her touch.*

*Oh how I yearn for those
nights with her and her alone.*

She's as sassy
as she is sublime
requiring nights
of adoration and worship
all the way from her
lips to her hips to
teasing her desire
through the use of
nothing but my fingertips.

All it takes is for
her to wear nothing
but a nibbled lip and
an oversized jumper
to leave me like a puddle
yearning for her to
wear the mark I
subtly yet ravenously
give her.

*It's not the monsters
under the bed
you have to
worry about
when you're
under the sheets
and she's in the
kinda mood.*

*Swell upon my
lips darling.
Pulsate at my touch.
Drown me completely
sweetheart as I'm
pretty sure there's
more to come.*

There's no stopping
a love like this.
The type to leave you
spent and breathless
gripping the sheets
head back eyes closed.
In awe of the sublime
emotion and ravenous hunger
and that's before we touch,
that's before we even embrace.
That's before the anticipation
gets the better of us.
Oh yes.
Let us love like this and
keep it as a story that we
can tell the grandkids one day.

*Oh that halo looks
great wrapped
around her wrists
as she wraps me
in her wings and
shows me exactly
what heaven
looks like.*

*I long for
bound wrists and
shackled ankles.
Wild hair wrapped
in my fist as our lips
meet in the first of
many passionate
kisses tonight.
Every inch of her teased
carefully
tenderly.
Ropes tight around
your submissive skin
and my eyes go wide
as I realise that you're
about to let me in.*

She could be as
feral as she likes
but we both know
as soon as I kiss
her neck she'll melt
and purr like a kitten.

She had a love
for fire
flannel
and fishnets

and I fell HARD!

Sebastian was right.
Everything is better
when she is wetter.
Take it from me.

*Sometimes you've
got to gently
caress her spine
spread her pages
and pore over her
chapters and footnotes
as if your life
depended on it.*

*She's the kinda girl
who could make
watching paint dry
really fucking exciting
whilst she whispers
everything that she
wants done to her
against it when
it's finished.*

*It's those adorable
and sweet looking girls
you've got to keep
your eye on
as they can fuck
shit up, smile,
do that thing with
their fingers and
get away with it
every damn time.*

With a wandering eye
she caught me gazing at
the stars. Wandering over
she sat with me and talked
for hours about the
constellations Greek
mythology and what would
happen if Phil had done a
better job whilst supervising
those pesky Raptors in
Jurassic Park.
As the silence came I found the
courage to ask for her name.
And to my surprise she replies
"I'll give you three guesses
and if you're correct I can bet
you'll be screaming it later.
Hell you'll be screaming it
if you're wrong."

*And like the most
succulent of
forbidden fruits
her peach was
intoxicating
a pure addiction
sweet on the lips
and worth every
single sugar high
and extreme low.*

She looked beautiful
as the moon light
hit her curves and
the bed sheets cling
to our skin amidst a
session of glorious sin.

*I swear that
an angel gets
its wings
every time
she gets
her own way*

Who would've thought
spanking her ass and
pulling her hair would
bring out the freak in her...

Surely they should
teach that shit
in school.

There she is....
The girl who
would rock
your world
and make every
single one of
your daydreams
WET!!!

*I'm a sucker for
the mark she left
on my chest,
a work of art
created during a
night of lust love and
desire right there
deep within my skin.*

*She's in the business
of pressing buttons
living life fully
and ravishing the
fuck out of me.*

*She's the girl
the devil herself
would sell her
soul for.*

*Her hips were
meant for shaking
as much as both
sets of her lips
were meant
for kissing.*

Is there anything
more intimate than
washing the sins
of the day right out
of your lover's hair
as you both melt into
each other creating
a feeling of peace and
wonderful tranquillity?!?

*With eyes filled
with wonder
and a kiss that
would smoulder
she would oft
leave me feeling
a little hot
under the collar.*

I'd always give
her a reason
to be bratty
and sassy
as I can't help
but melt
when she whispers
"Make me"

She has a penchant
for love and lust
and some naughty
whispered lullabies.

She may look
like the
girl next door
but by Christ
can she fuck
like a porn star.

*I long for those
nights by the fire
snuggled up with
my hand down
her pants stoking
her desire....*

whilst she reads a book.

*She was madness
and chaos wrapped
in the finest denim
and wearing quite
he alluring and
kissable smirk*

I've heard her
being described
as a little
firecracker
but
trust me
that
raven vixen
is like pure
fucking dynamite.

*If you were expecting
to find milkshakes
in that girl's backyard
you'll be in for a
bit of a shock
as all you'll find are
handcuffs whiskey
a stripper pole and
that sex kitten
running amok.*

Oh fuck. Kitten...
I live for the nights
when our lips meet
and you drag me in
deeply so that I
can drink every
inch of you in.

*My mother warned
me about girls
like you
but she didn't
prepare me for
how fast and
hard I would
fall for you.*

*Her kiss was scintillating
her ass could be described
as sizzling, those legs for days
often walked through my mind
and her heart was the greatest
thing I could ever find.*

She's the girl
who would drive
a Saint straight
to sin with her
seductive words
her bombshell looks
and that wicked grin.

*She may be cute
but when she is
in that mood
you can bet
your ass she
wouldn't stop
until she had
corrupted you.*

*There's just something
about the way she
would wear her
heart on her sleeve
and her neck in my teeth.*

*It's not always
about sex and
safe words
sometimes
she plays my
ass like a drum.*

*She wasn't afraid
of the dark as she
knew exactly
what kind of
shit she would do
when the lights
were off.*

I'm a sucker for
the way she fucks
me when she's
frustrated,
it's like I haven't got
a choice and
yup
I
Love
That.

*The only prize
worth coming
second for
is her smile
and carnal
satisfaction.*

Oh kitten...
Don't look at me
with that tone
of voice.
I know exactly
what you want.

*She's as irresistible
as she is insatiable
and I couldn't help
but want to taste
those wet lips
24/7*

Yes she's a handful
but it's her dainty hands
that excite me.

*Her lips and hips
would turn every
single Saint into
a ravenous sinner.*

Her sweet release
was like Holy water
baptising my lips
and chin amidst
a night of passion
and sweet delicious
and totally
satisfying sin.

Her lips were loaded.
Her words like soft bullets
as they penetrate my
already open heart.
Her soft voice ringing
in my ears as they whisper
exactly where the night
is headed, as she whispers
watch she wants going
forward.
Taking my hand in hers
toying with each finger
I notice a coy smirk form
as she decides where she
wants each digit to go.

Her eyes told
a story that
her lips tried
to hold back.
The ink in
her veins
bubbling and
boiling filled
with a plethora
of adventures
filled with
emotion
passion
and
erotic pleasure.

She's a little witchy too...

*She was mythical,
magical, and
marvellous.
Even with both feet
rooted firmly on
the ground.*

*I have no doubts
that she's mystical
and magical as
the spell she cast
has me feeling
some kind of way.*

She was a temptress
an enchantress
and one hell of a
fucking badass.

She was born of witches
and raised by wolves
so you would be foolish
to attempt to fuck with her.

*She is magic amidst
the mundane.
She is an extraordinary spirit
amidst ordinary souls.
She is a sultry sensual vixen
with a penchant for
intoxicating thoughts.
She is my muse.
She is the light of my life.
She is pure mystery
and I don't know how
but somehow she's mine.*

*She is part princess
and definitely
part Maleficent.
So trust me,
she may look innocent
but she'll fuck you up.*

She was as mad as Alice and twice as adventurous.

She is cut from
the same cloth
as witches and
warlocks, and
that could be seen
in that special
sensual and sexual
power she has over me

*I can't help
but fall hard
when her
spooky ass
seduces my
geeky heart.*

*Some say she was
born of the storm.
I say she is the storm
with her loose lips
having the ability to
sink ships and knowing
the same could be
said about her hips.*

*Spooky girls do it
better by casting
spells with their
eyes without ever
having to think twice.*

*Her magic may
be practical.
But that ass is
fantastical.*

I gave my heart
to her witchy ass
and this muggle
couldn't be happier.

*Keep that chin up
sweetheart....*

*There's spells
to be cast.*

*She brought the
sun back into
my life and
that's why I
worship her
full moon.*

*She told me tales
of white knights
and dragons and
how they weren't
for her, not since
the day she decided
to save herself.*

*She would redefine
what you thought
a bewitching badass
could be.......*

Trust me!

She's as innocent
as she is witchy
a complete contradiction
with an enticing smile
an alluring intelligence
and a penchant for
such sweet corruption.

Oh!
She's give you a
reason to believe
in magic, and it
don't matter
if you like it or not.

She was a sucker
for rose's
dark romances
and fucking
amidst the crystals
on her altar.

She's such a pretty
little witch
wearing nothing but
a nymphish grin and plaid

She would be
the leader of
the pack
an alpha
a badass
with the soul
of a wolf and
a warrior's heart

I fell for a witch
I fell for a reader
I may not believe
in much, but I
believe in her

*She was
magical
mystical
mysterious
mine!*

She hid her
secrets with
the stars
as she knew
they would
keep them
until she found
a worthy ear
in which to
whisper them in.

*I fell for the
girl with a
vintage soul
a love for witchcraft
and a sinners tongue.*

She's as sassy
as she is magical.
Bending smoke,
water and my desires
in-between her
slender fingertips.

*Some wish upon
a star, and I make
wishes upon her eyes
and still get the
desired effect.*

*She rolled in
like a storm
wrapped in
black lace,
and left like
a hurricane
with a wild
smile on
my face.*

She may be spiritual
but fuck with her
and she'll become
stabby as fuck!

*Keep your eyes
on the girl with
that witchy fire
in her smile.*

Trust me.

*You're not going
to want to
miss a thing.*

*She's the kinda
girl who would
brave and chase
the storm, and
come back with
the eye as her prize.*

*And like a tale
as old as time
and a song as
old as rhyme
she was the
intoxicating beauty
to my insatiable
and ravenous beast.*

She had a love
for poetry
mythology
and being
herself
unconditionally.

Don't let that
halo fool you
as it's those
black wings
dark humour
and those
legs for days
that will turn
every king into
a speechless jester.

*She deserved MAGIC
and wouldn't settle
for anything less than that.*

Even on a mediocre day
she's magical as fuck.

*That resting witch face
of hers is a sight to behold.*

*Gazing into those eyes
I'm spellbound
entranced and attracted
to those sweet alluring lips.*

What do you mean
unicorns aren't real?
I'm pretty sure the
girl with the
resting smirk face
is magical
and supernatural
as fuck
and rainbows
do indeed illuminate
from that sublime
peach of her behind.

*She's not an angel
that sits on any tree*

*she's a goddess in
leather and denim
that desires worship
from you on your knees.*

*With moonlight
in her eye
the stardust in
her smile
oozed forth with
a divine need to
be kissed before
she gets up to
some red hot
witchy shit.*

*Sometimes the
princess saves
herself
tames the dragon
and lives
badassily
ever after.*

*Her favourite thing
to do was cast spells
do some witchy shit
and create as many
awkward boners
as she could.*

*When the moon
is full just sit
back and watch
her bloom as
her eyes teach
the stars how
to sparkle.*

*I found beauty
in her darkness
but fell in love
with her
blinding light.*

*She's as alluring
as she is exhilarating.
An adorable contradiction
with a warm heart
bewitching eyes
an addictive kiss
and an absolutely
charismatic and
mystical soul.*

*She had a
deep love for
crystals
candles and
witchcraft.
And I
well
I
had deep love
for her and
whatever made
her happy.*

*She was born
from the flames
which is why
her heart will
never be cold.*

It's her divine light
warm heart
and bewitching mind
that makes her
Goddess tiers
of beautiful.

She laid her roots
in the autumn
so she could be
strong and
unbeatable when
August ends.

*Once upon a time
the princess said
NO!!
The End!*

You should see
her under the
new moon.
You should watch
her come out
of her shell and
become quite
the divine vixen
that is no longer
afraid of the
Hell that
surrounds her.

*You'll find her
amidst rose's
crystals and candles
and you can bet
your ass that you'll
find her there with
a huge smile on her face.*

She wanted to
teach the world
how to dance
so she started with
the fairies and
pixies at the
bottom of her garden.

If she has a love
for chokers candles
and crystals you
should know
there is no way
in heaven or hell
that her bewitching
ass will ever be tamed
or forced back in her shell.

*She was like
lightening in
a bottle.
Extremely
volatile
when caged
but dangerously
beautiful when
she is left
to strike!*

There's this girl
and the fire
in her heart
would teach
the phoenix
how to rise.

*Her vibe is different
when the moon is full
and she knows exactly
what she wants to do.*

Oh my dark angel.
Build up that sass.
Shine that halo
and go kick some ass.

She had a rare soul
so much so
that once held
close to your chest
you would never
want to let go.

There's this girl
and once she's
fallen in love
with the moon
she knows deep
within her soul
that will be a
bond that will
never be broken

*Even Hell wouldn't
be ready for the
fire that burns
deeply inside her.*

*She turned her
magic up all the
way to eleven*

*and lived
HAPPILY
EVER
AFTER.*

Oh Darling

Oh darling
my heart may be pure
but I sure do love it
when you absolutely
corrupt me
completely
in the bedroom.

Oh darling
the romantic
in me will
whisper everything
I'll do for you,
yet the beast
will firmly say
exactly

WHAT
HE'LL
DO!

Oh darling.
Your sass is
showing!!
And my God is
it beautiful

*Oh darling I'm
going to love you
so hard and so fast
that your butterflies
wouldn't know
what hit them.*

Oh darling
if I were to
bare my teeth
would you
dare to fill them.

Oh darling
you have the right
to remain silent,

but when the
handcuffs come out
I want you to be
as loud as possible!

Oh darling
dinners in the oven.
There are Nerf guns
on the table.
Meet me outside the
blanket fort.
We're going to war.

Oh darling
be gentle with
my heart and
I'll show you how
fucking beastly
I can be.

Oh darling,
please believe me
when I say
my mind is
your playground
as much as
my body is your canvas.

Oh darling
I would do anything
for that alluring heart
and masterpiece of
an arse of yours.

Oh darling
Pull my beard
and spank my ass.
I've been such
a good boy.

Oh darling
I worry and think
about you all
the time.
Even when you've
told me not to
as that's what I do.

Oh darling
Intoxicate this
mind of mine
and you can
maul my body
anytime.

Oh darling
Do you feel that kitten?
That's you twisting
my arm with those
puppy dog eyes
and uberlly angelic smile.

Oh darling
you don't have to
say anything.
Not whilst your
eyes give you away.

Oh darling
Love me like the
savage I know
you can be.

Oh darling
I promise that
what we have
in the here and now
we'll have in the
there and future too.

*Oh darling
you're going to have
to be loud enough
so the angels know
how much I
worship you.*

Oh darling
you know I
promise thee
that you'll never
feel mundane but
always extraordinary.

Oh darling
your eyes are
like fire, as I
must admit
I melt every time
I gaze upon them.

Oh darling
don't be afraid
to have your say.
Drop the microphone
and walk away.

*Oh darling
set your lips to stun
as my knees are
already weak.*

Oh darling
don't be shy
as we both know
damn well that
your smile is
too beautiful
to hide.

Oh darling
time spent doing
nothing with you
is never wasted.

*Oh darling
lets wrap each
other in tinsel
and get a little
"festive"*

Oh darling
there may only
be seven deadly sins
but tonight we're
making a few more.

*Oh darling
kiss me like
you miss me
and maul me
like you love me.*

Oh darling
what an honour
it would be
to hold you from
when the day ends
to when a new day
begins.......
And repeat for
eternity.

*Oh darling
whatever we have
I'm pretty sure
the world needs
more of.
So yeah
why don't we go
and give it to them.*

Oh darling
I'm not mad about
the bad things you
could possibly do,
but I'm definitely
bat shit mad and
nose over tail
for you.

Oh darling
Come here.
Let's eat junk food
binge a new series
and order stuff
we don't need
but really fucking want!

Oh darling
if you ever want
to shut me up
just tease my neck
and kiss me hard.
Yeah
mhmmm
sighs
That works
EVERY
SINGLE
TIME!!

Oh darling
send nudes,
or failing that
send me pictures
of your kitty.

That's how you
sext right?!?

Oh darling
may the light
never dim
in your heart.

Oh darling
in the immortal
words of Bob Ross
will you be
my happy little tree.

Oh darling...
Sometimes
if you want me
to do that thing
you want you're
going to have to
bite me harder.

*Oh darling
how I ache
to take photos
of all the magical
things we do in
all the extraordinary
places we go to.*

*Oh darling
lets go for
one of those
coffees that
leads to sex.
I'm a lil thirsty.*

*Oh darling
you won't be
punished for
being sassy
but I might
reward you with
a bitten neck
and one hell of a
night to remember.*

*Oh darling
we both know
there's nothing
wrong with a
little sin right
before breakfast.*

Oh darling
why should we
rock around the
Christmas tree
when I could get
on my knees
and pleasure you
under it?!?

Oh darling
lrust me
when I say
I'll give you
many reasons
as to why we
should stay in
bed all day.

*Oh darling
your spirit
is showing
and yup
it's glorious
rendering me
speechless.*

Oh darling
the bigger the hair
the more there is
to share as it gets
wrapped in my fist
as we nibble and suck
and lick and fuck
the day away.

Oh darling...
Don't underestimate
the power of your lips
and that delicious
addictive intoxicating kiss.

Oh darling
please never change,
you're such a
delightful riot
just the way you are.

*Oh darling
sometimes it's
a great idea
to play a game
of hands down pants
just to see who
will come first.*

*Oh darling
roses were
designed to
bloom in the wild,*

AND SO ARE YOU.

*Oh darling
I would love
you in secret.
But I have a
BIG MOUTH!*

Oh darling
there's a devil
in all of us
and mine wants
to be deep inside you.

Oh darling
If you must leave me

leave me not as
you found me,

leave me changed
for the better,

leave me knowing
what it felt like
to be loved,

leave me feeling there
is some good in this world.

Oh darling.
If you do leave me
please don't leave me broken.

She Had Me At.....

She had me at
"Take those pants off"

She had me at
"Yippykiyay
motherfucker"

She had me at
"Your mother sucks
cocks in hell"

She had me at
"I'm too old
for this shit"

She had me at
"SUCK IT"

She had me at
"Sit the fuck down
and do as you're told"

She had me at
"Houston....
We have a problem"

She had me at
"Life uh...
Finds a way"

She had me at
"It can't rain
all the time"

*She had me at
"Punch it Chewie"*

She had me at
"Don't cross
the streams"

*She had me at
"What's in
the box?"*

*She had me at
"I'm afraid you're
just too damn loud"*

She had me at
"Beetlejuice
Beetlejuice...
Nope not saying that
a third time"

*She had me at
"We are the weirdo's mister"*

*She had me at
"Thundercats
Hooooooooh"*

She had me at
"Autobots...
Roll out!"

*She had me at
"You were supposed
to destroy the Sith,
not join them."*

She had me at
"Have you ever danced
with the Devil in the pale
moonlight?"

She had me at
"My teeth and ambitions
are bared...
Be prepared"

She had me at
"Goonies never
say die!"

She had me at
"1. 2.
Freddie's coming
for you!"

She had me at
"I'll get you next time
Gadget
next time!"

She had me at
"Johnny 5
is alive!"

She had me at
"Where we're going
we don't need roads."

She had me at
"You scruffy looking
Nerf herder"

She had me at
"It's SHOWTIME"

*She had me at
"Do you smell
what the Rock
is cooking?"*

She had me at
"Run Forrest run!"

*She had me at
"Suck me beautiful"*

She had me at
"I love you 3000"

She had me at
"Taste the rainbow"

She had me at
"Why do we
fall Bruce?"

She had me at
"Only Sith deal
in absolutes."

She had me at
"I have the high ground."

She had me at
"You didn't say
the magic word
Ah Ah Ah."

*She had me at
"Don't go into
the long grass."*

She had me at
"There is no Dana.
Only Zuul!!"

*She had me at
"She was a small town girl
living in a lonely world."*

She had me at
"Hold my beer!"

She had me at
"It's one for the money
and two for the show"

She had me at
"I bless the rains
down in Africa"

She had me at
"I bet you look good
on the dance floor."

She had me at
"I did it all
for the nookie!"

She had me at
"I'm never gonna
give you up,
I'm never gonna
let you down."

She had me at
"I'm gonna uptown
funk you up.....
Don't believe me
just watch."

She had me at
"Twinkle twinkle
you fucking star!"

She had me at
"Stand and
deliver!"

She had me at
"I've got a
machine gun.
Ho ho ho!"

She had me at
"You've got class,
you could be
a contender"

She had me at
"THIS IS THE WAY!"

She had me at
"It's so fluffy
I'm gonna die!"

She had me at
"You scumbag
you maggot"

She had me at
"Say what one
more time!"

*She had me at
"Keep the change
you filthy animal."*

She had me at
"We are GROOT!"

*She had me at
"May the force
be with you!"*

Acknowledgements

Mum and Dad.... Forever missed, forever loved. You will always always always be my anchor and rock!

To Rich, Lindsey, Tracy, the kids and better halves and the rest of the family. Without you I would live with my head in the clouds.

To Wayne: the best mate who is solely responsible for my caffeine addiction and many wild nights that I have probably mostly forgotten.

To Sarah: See.... I remembered to add you again.

To Luke: Oh Mr Bomber it looks like Mr Ryan wrote a book

Big thanks to Dave, Sian, Saskia, and the folks at Game in Haverfordwest.

To all the poets I've met through social media. You guys rule.
Keep doing what you do.

Thanks go to the dudes Dan Bailey, Eric Keegan, The Devils Chaos, Rex, Dave Smith, Thad, and Ceri "Daybrkr" Collins . Clinks glass. Cheers.

A big thank you to Broms, J Warren Welch, The Captain, Pico, Matt Spenser, Patrick Moore, Matt Baker, Ryan Morrow, The Bee Bar Barman, and A. Effing, you guys always make me want to be a better writer.

A great big thank you to my poet in crime my banter buddy my best friend and author of Redemption Laura Wheeler. I am eternally grateful for your unconditional support and kicks up the ass.

And to everyone who picked up a copy of my previous anthologies Words like Whiskey Shots, The First 100, and Rayban and Red Eyes and or picked up a copy of the collaborative efforts Roses and Red Eyes and The Raven Queen and the Smuggler
also a huge thanks to anyone who has taken the time out of the day to like a bunch a shit of mine on the ole Instagram.

About the author

H.S. Smiles is the alter ego of a hopelessly romantic small town Welshman with a coffee addiction, big hands, flat arse and a generous heart.
H.S. Smiles used to find home amidst crowds and on stages but since his bout of writers block and stage fright he has found home in his armchair writing and watching reruns of old comedy shows and Star Wars movies.
One day H.S. Smiles will show his face to the world again, but today my friends is not that day.

More works by the author

Words like Whiskey Shots
The First 100
Raybans and Red Eyes
Roses and Red Eyes with Laura wheeler
The Raven Queen and the Smuggler with Laura wheeler

Social Media

Instagram: @hansolossmile
Facebook:
https://www.facebook.com/hansolossmile

Printed in Great Britain
by Amazon